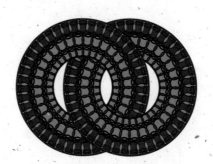

The Baby Book

The Baby Book

Robin Silbergleid

CavanKerry ◈ Press LTD.

CavanKerry Press Ltd.
Fort Lee, New Jersey
www.cavankerrypress.org

Publisher's Cataloging-in-Publication
(Provided by Quality Books, Inc.)
Silbergleid, Robin.
[Poems. Selections]
The baby book / Robin Silbergleid. -- First edition.
pages cm
Poems.
ISBN 978-1-933880-58-7
I. Title.
PS3619.I542A6 2015   811'.6
QBI15-600124

Cover photographs: petri dishes © 2015 by Fotoedukacja;
baby image © Cathy Yeulet, 123rf.com
Cover and interior text design by Gregory Smith
First Edition 2015, Printed in the United States of America

The Baby Book is the eleventh title of CavanKerry's Literature of Illness imprint. LaurelBooks are fine collections of poetry and prose that explore the many poignant issues associated with confronting serious physical and/or psychological illness.

CavanKerry Press is grateful for the support it receives from the New Jersey State Council on the Arts.

Also by Robin Silbergleid

POETRY

Pas de Deux: Prose and Other Poems (2006)

Frida Kahlo, My Sister (2014)

PROSE

Texas Girl: A Memoir (2014)

The first—killing the Angel in the House—I think I solved. She died. But the second, telling the truth about my own experiences as a body, I do not think I solved. I doubt that any woman has solved it yet.

—Virginia Woolf, "Professions for Women"

Contents

III

IV

V

The Baby Book

Infertility Sestina

This is how it goes: say you want a baby
say you are twenty-seven & alone,
as in uncoupled, there is no father
in this equation: you read *Taking Charge of Your Fertility*
keep charts & graphs, cycle days & symptoms. Months
tracking cervical fluid, basal body temperature. Patient,

you wait, you bleed, you write; you are more patient
than you thought possible. Everyone is having babies
but you. You read messages online, every month
someone else gets pregnant; you feel alone,
certain of the diagnosis—628.9 Infertility
(female, unknown)—although you are only lacking a father's

DNA. Your child will have a donor, not a father—
the sample shipped on dry ice to the clinic. Patience,
your doctor says, you could be "Fertile
Myrtle." After the procedure, you go to the Baby
Gap, buy teeny white socks & onesies, a lone
purple cap. You imagine dressing your newborn months

from now. Cycles tick by in prenatals & pills, six months
of progesterone supplements & finally *positive*. "I'm a father!"
the nurse jokes when she draws your blood; she left you alone
with your legs in the air two weeks ago, your patient
check-out form on the counter, & in those quiet moments a baby
started to take shape, simple kiss of egg & sperm & bam.

In the fertility

clinic waiting room you skim pamphlets on male factor infertility
& the magazines that have sat there for months
mocking you, *Working Mother, American Baby,*
Fit Pregnancy. It is your nurse, not some father-
to-be who sits with you for the sonogram, patiently
searching for the embryo, the heartbeat, & then she leaves you alone

to put on your clothes, to drive home, more lonely
than you have ever been. Not pregnant, your chart says, infertile:
blighted ovum, missed miscarriage, D&C at 11w4d. Patient
will call to schedule follow-up appointment in a month.

This is how it goes. You wanted to be a single mother
but there is a black hole in your uterus, not a baby.

I Will Name My Daughter Hannah

"Do you want a Tic-Tac? Do you want a Lifesaver or a butterscotch?"
Grandma's pocketbook is a candy store, a pharmacy, a spare room. She
always carries change for a pony ride outside the K-Mart or a phone
call from the bus station, a container of Tylenol and baby aspirin, a
travel-sized box of Kleenex. She always carries an umbrella and pair
of L'Eggs in beige. There's even room for a Game Boy and emergency
shoes. She's from the generation of *always be prepared* and a trip to
the beauty parlor on Saturday afternoon. She could call him from
Newark and say, "I'm going to *shul*," board a plane with a passport
stamped to Jerusalem, Tel Aviv. Even a farm girl from New Brunswick
knows to keep her papers with her at all times: birth certificate, life
insurance policy, quarterly reports from the stockbroker. Not a purse
or a backpack or even a handbag; it's her *pocketbook*, a word unmoored
from denotation, one of those heavy, clunky nouns I might have told
her in first grade is *com-pound*:

Now, at twenty-seven, I look it up in the OED—available online—
at my mahogany desk that's really the kitchen table where my uncle,
as a child, did his math homework and carved his name in the wood,
drinking a glass of milk and sneaking cookies from a Fiestaware
plate. I think about the way that history exists in objects that have
no value in her twenty-page will, like Liz Claiborne accessories,
cans of cling peaches and tunafish. I promise to treasure family
stories like Tastykakes in the cupboard, tell them to the daughter
who will bear her name. And I start carrying a needle and a spool of
pink thread, ready to sew buttons on tiny sweaters or mend holes in
cotton socks, just in case.

Curiosity

*I'm better at these lies that I've manufactured than I am at the lies
I'm living.*

—after the film *Playing by Heart* (1998)

You keep checking out odd books from the library—
about childbirth, about conjoined twins and cooking
for one, how to decorate a nursery in seven easy steps.
No, not odd, just unexpected. On the cover
of *What to Expect When You're Expecting,*
a woman in a red smock rests
an open book on the pillow of her belly,
rocking, rocking. You wonder
if the spiky-haired girl at the checkout counter
will ask *when's the baby due?*
a game of impersonation
like the man in the movie who pretended to be
a different person each night for a week
but each character always broke
his wife's unsuspecting heart. The best lies
always contain a kernel of curiosity and desire,
so last week, under the oversized sweatshirt
swiped from your friend the Harvard grad,
you padded your waist until you could pass,
then went to the grocery store, bought
milk and juice and vitamin pills.
Simple, like carrying a pair of toe shoes

in your backpack or the complete poems
of Wordsworth on a warm summer afternoon.
People see what they want to see
anyway, and you're not interested in being
who you're supposed to be anymore,
cloistered and serious, dyeing your hair
the blackest black for the thrill
of being someone new. So you dream
of names like India Carmel and Samara Blythe,
try on foreign accents like secondhand clothes,
imagine being a dancer, a mother,
a private eye. You dream the child
reinvents you, cell by glorious cell.

Chaste Tree

Once, it was given to curb the sex drives
of medieval monks.
                              So the name:
agnus-castus, its aftertaste foul enough
to dampen the longings of Roman brides,

their husbands rowing toward Messana
to fight. Who would want to kiss
their sulphury mouths?
                              It doesn't quell
my desire for you, sweet child, this diurnal
potion of leaf-colored powder and orange juice.

Take it, the healer says, with raspberry tea
and wild yam.
                              She kneads my uterus
with strong hands, relaxing muscle
clenched around what it won't hold, the smallest speck
of a child, drowning in mucous and the inevitable.
My belly contracts and then softens.
She doubles the tincture, says, next month

the egg will come on time. Each

morning, Chaste Tree and Vitamin C.
A pill. A prayer. A single-celled wish.

The Childless Women
Talk about Frida Kahlo

i

Vecina, my friend says, look
at this Kahlo:

>   the head that should rest
>   on the mother's pillow lolling between bent knees,
>   dark-haired, limp-necked, Frida giving birth to herself.

Yes, I say, yes yes.

And this one:

>   big-bellied in the Michigan hospital,
>   holding her fetus like a balloon on a string, the bones
>   of her hips wide as elephant ears, uterus in shades
>   of lavender under the bed. Smokestacks flank
>   the bed, big enough to hold three lost children,
>   the mother's body, open, on display.

Yes.

>   Frida, bedridden, paints the miscarriage, turns
>   herself into a mother nursing her infant, her Diegocito.
>   She drinks tequila, sleeps in a morphine haze, wakes.
>   Frida, childless, paints. Frida, in ribbon and lace,
>   Tehuana with a monkey in her arms instead of a child.

Frida,

>   all I could think of—

In the Blue House at Coyoacán, Frida pretends to be a mother, baby
asleep in a glass womb, taking in formaldehyde through waxy skin.
His dolly siblings are envious, open-eyed in their tiny beds. At night,
she sings them lullabies; when they sleep, she reads about pregnancy
and babycare, palming the new bowl of her belly. This winter

her son would have been three, but he's somewhere in Detroit,
a blot on a sheet at the Henry Ford Hospital. He came out of her
in pieces, purple and brown stains on her underwear.
She makes sure her babies are clothed and tended, hair brushed
and bodies washed. She'd amputate if she had to,

to keep them safe. It's not her child that sleeps in the jar
on the bedside table. Sometimes she wonders whose it is,
how much it was wanted. Or maybe it wasn't—
with its curved spine and pointed head—she wonders how long
its mother struggled to birth it, how long its skull was wedged

under the pubis. Sometimes she thinks about opening her legs
and pushing the child back inside, splitting her vagina a second
time, and when the blood comes, pushing it out with each pang.
She's given birth so many times, a jumble of bloody sheets
she can't remember—

iii

Months later, the only way
I know to describe it:

                the bathroom

like a painting by Frida Kahlo, fat
spatters of blood, the anguished body of

a woman who will never be a mother
in the throes of birth.
                 When contractions

come, blood pulses between my thighs,
clots of something I can't name

pool in the tub. One by one by one
I gather them in my hands.

I draw the child I won't have
along the porcelain.

Postcards from the Clinic (#1)

In the waiting room
I read *Working Mother* and
grade blue book exams.

Three Aprils

i

Her hand between my thighs

the cruelest month

talking about Eliot, Joyce,
her hand cupping
my uterus, an overripe pear. Outside

it snows white petals:
blossoms from Bradford pears
and fat flakes far too late
in the season. It was snowing that day

when the word *abnormal* took shape
and multiplied under the microscope.

Her hand
on the speculum
her hand
with the hole punch. She cuts
soft bits of me like paper

and I bleed.

ii

I wonder if I'll ever be able to explain
what happened,
how blood ran rivulets
down my legs, pooled on the white tile floor
stuck in the grout. I wonder if I should put
one

on the line indicating pregnancy on the medical form.
The word *miscarriage*
cramps. The cervix opens

cut away like a paper snowflake. I wonder
if there will be anything left
to keep the child inside.

iii

April, another waiting
room, another doctor's hand
and me

stirrupped. *Chaste Tree*
I tell her, *Vitamin C.*
Her hand
on the pen now, writing.

Normal, she says,

and I think of the pills
lined up next to the juice glass
the thermometer (pink) on the bedside table
the box of test sticks (blue) in the bathroom.

She tells me to write
all of it
draw circles and connect the dots.
She tells me

the shape of a baby

is a word on white paper
a word I'm not ready to name.

Refuse

I can tell what day it is from the trashcan.
Household psychic, rifling through crushed paper
cups, pillows of tissue, sanitary pads wrapped in blue
like bedrolls piled in the back of an SUV. Test kits
tossed out like sporks, spent and unwanted.

Today is the fourteenth day. I've cleaned
the cats' box with gloved hands, brought the bags
to the dumpster. Later, my neighbors will put out
pizza boxes, bottles of longneck beer. How
it smells. The breakfast I couldn't eat rises up.

It smells like loss. It smells like desire.

The Phlebotomist

When people ask, she says she's a modern-day vampire, drawing vials of blood and stopping them with rubber caps. It's how she lives, feeding off strangers to buy groceries and pay Cable One. Sometimes it's a girl who needs a pregnancy test, sometimes a man in a blue suit worried about HIV. She knows all the codes, diagnoses for anticoagulation therapy and infertility, the woman who comes in at the same time every month with lovely veins, boxes for progesterone and prothrombin time checked on her form. The answers swirl in her blood, illegible as food coloring or fingerpaint. All she can do is pray. All she can do is roll the dark tubes in her hand.

The Fertility Patient

628.9 Infertility (unknown)
> For six months, numerical codes

628.9 Infertility (unknown)
> on insurance forms. The doctor

628.9 Infertility (unknown)
> writes in blue ink, her certain

628.9 Infertility (unknown)
> hand. She prescribes pills:

628.9 Infertility (unknown)
> serophene, baby aspirin, progesterone.

628.9 Infertility (unknown)
> The nurse fills vials with blood—six

V72.4 Pregnancy, unconfirmed
> seven, eight. The nurse makes her pee

V72.4 Pregnancy, unconfirmed
> on a stick. In a cup. The nurse draws

V72.4 Pregnancy, unconfirmed
> another vial. The doctor asks

V22.2 Intrauterine pregnancy
> her to open her legs, inserts a catheter,

V22.2 Intrauterine pregnancy
> a probe. On the monitor, the sac

V23.9 Prenatal care, high-risk
> comes into focus, black, tiny. The doctor says

V23.9 Prenatal care, high-risk
> *we can't rule out an ectopic.* The doctor asks

V23.9 Prenatal care, high-risk

        her to open her legs, inserts a probe.

632 Missed abortion

        Says, *the sac is bigger, but there's still nothing*

632 Missed abortion

        inside. They offer injections, surgery.

632 Missed abortion

        They offer Kleenex from a cardboard box.

632 Missed abortion

        The fertility patient thinks,

632 Missed abortion

        this is my life, my blood—

628.9 Infertility (unknown)

The Missed Miscarriage

*It is impossible to gauge the depth of grief either by the size of the coffin
or the circumstances of the loss.*

—Kim Kluger-Bell, *Unspeakable Losses*

For twelve weeks I lugged him
everywhere I went, belly
swollen, nine pounds
this grief, the weight of a child
smaller than a grain of rice.
On the sonogram, my uterus
a dark cavern, empty. This
is what desire looks like:
in the nurse's station, she drew
tubes of blood, papers saying I knew
the drug could cause a birth defect,
methotrexate, for killing
unwanted cells.
                    My son
was wanted, the placenta
that nourished him kept growing:
cake baked with too much yeast.

The nurse waited for me
to pull down my black tights
to lean over the table
shifting my weight to my right.

For days my body ached
with knowledge of what we had done,
the child she helped me conceive
and then took away.
                    After,
my body made milk for him—
if she hadn't stopped it,
it would have let him swallow me whole.

The Baby Doctor

Her patient (*30 y.o. WF*) cries over the phone. Every day when she calls to check up. She imagines the girl in a four-poster bed with a cat. Flannel pajamas. A stack of books, Sylvia Plath and Virginia Woolf. She thinks of her daughter, upstairs, practicing cursive. After the surgery, the vacant look in the girl's eyes. She'd refused anesthesia, said she needed the experience, eyes closed on the other side of the white sheet, both of them listening to the beep beep beep of the monitor, how it slowed with each careful breath. How she wanted to hold the girl's hand instead of a curette. She didn't cry then. But that awful morning they couldn't find the heartbeat on the sonogram (*dx: missed abortion, 7w2d*) and every afternoon when she calls. A few tears and a stifled sob. She thinks about her patient when she drives her daughter to ballet practice, the way her collarbones jutted through the wide neck of the hospital gown. How she wants to wrap her in cotton blankets, warm chocolate milk on the stove. She prescribes more antibiotics, a stronger analgesic, and she drives, gloved hands gripping the wheel.

I Draw My Doctor a Picture

A red print like a butterfly hinging its wings—

the simile makes
what is happening to me
beautiful, a girl
in the bathroom checking

for bloodstains. How many
times?
       It began at twelve

I stuffed paperthin tissue in my pants
and ignored it.

These days it's all
I think about, shades of pink, brown, red

like the paints I mixed in art class.
These are colors I know
how to make, how to add a tinge
of white, a drop of black. When

the doctor says, *tell me*

about the bleeding, I have nothing
but metaphor. It was a butterfly

it was a bucketful of blackberries
it was raindrops on pavement
at the beginning of a storm.

After the Miscarriage, My Doctor Speaks

One month since she touched me, her hand a hushed prayer against my forehead, a spoon that scooped my son like an avocado, overly ripe. I can't stop looking. Blue veins and freckled skin, thin fingers around a blue Bic pen, the kind I wrote with at eight, when the only certain thing was the teacher's hand. Another blue X on the checkout form, a list of blood tests, another prescription. She toys with her necklace, sits back in the burgundy chair.

"When?" I ask.

"When you stop dreaming of blackberries."

II

Miscarriage (3)

—after the film *Frida* (2002)

i

Here again::
        Three women:
fancy drinks with a pink parasols,
endless pots of Chinese tea.

The air around me smells
of nausea and nameless grief.
(Garlic, I think, ginger). Now
again, she begins

and the words
mother   baby   hospital
and the words, they
collect on the table
like used dishes, and I am there
thirty years ago, three pounds
(smaller than a Sunday chicken)
eight ounces

and here all at once,
birthday for a child who shouldn't have been:

my mother gowned
in a sterile room, a doll's bottle

in her shaking hand, seven weeks
early and none too soon

and here, now, my mother
with her grownup girl, me
drinking pink drinks
because I'm alive
and, oh,
            oh, oh—

ii

Once I collected fortunes
and favorite numbers, thirty
and the year of the rat, used
tissues lint my pockets

and my mother and my aunt
who won't stop talking

I wanted to tell you I'm sorry
about the baby, sorry you lost

and the baby who won't be
sits heavy in my pelvis
the placenta that tried so hard still
pumping blood to his stumped cells.

It all bleeds together—

Frida Kahlo, the actress, me
writing *(how many miscarriages?)*
a crimson tub, a blood-stained sheet
(he came out of me in pieces)
this thing that hasn't happened yet—

an image from a painting, a movie set,
the diary of a woman between.

Birth Stories

This is the closest we've come
in thirty years, here
over fried mushrooms and syrupy Coke,
the charbroiled smell of somebody's cigarette
clinging to my hair. *A midwife*—
the word catches in her throat, an infant
trapped in the vise of her mother's hips—
wouldn't have been able to save you.

My hand finds its way to that secret curve,
that softness below my navel where,
maybe, the child sleeps. I want to ask
what it was like to have loss
open like a rhetorical question
for weeks in the NICU. *Was it like*
if, after twenty-four hours or something,
you would know? The child's sentence
punctuated, certain. I've seen
the pictures, the mother masked, the preemie
behind glass, fed from a doll's bottle.
I know about the car rides
to and from the hospital
long December afternoons—
what the sky looked like
over the arboretum, trees lining Route 53.

This is all she ever says.
I want more, want
to know what it felt like
to see the child tubed on the table still
warm with the smell of her womb.

My stomach turns. What's been
stuck rises up, threatens
to spill over like a glass of soda
poured too soon. I say
I've been doing research. *For a story*
I add. For the story that is my life.

Lisle, Illinois, November 1972

My father eats cold chop suey,
props the carton on the slow curve
of his stomach. It matches my mother's.
She, folding clothes in the nursery, thinks
another six weeks to paint,
to pick out names—she calls me *Robin,*
harbinger of spring. Just past Thanksgiving,
she knows what she has to be thankful for,
the neighbor upstairs, the baby on the way.
1,000 miles from home, she feels like
a pioneer woman on an abandoned homestead.
She tells herself she's being ridiculous, my father
watching TV in the next room. He has
a law degree, works for the government. Each day
she drives him to work so she can use
their one brown car, buy groceries, pink dresses.
Each day she walks the dog
around the parking lot, gets the mail.
Sometimes there's a letter from New Jersey,
California. Sometimes there's a magazine—
Women's Day or *Ladies' Home Journal*.
This is our home now, she tells the dog,
the child, as her waters break on the sidewalk.

Postcards from the Clinic (#2)

My doctor comes out
and kisses her son while I
wait to miscarry.

Metaphor

There is no poetry
in loss, I refuse

to indulge, to shimmer
half-light of Texas winter

where glass sparkled the floor
like precious gems. No—

the language of loss
is silence, heavy

as the forty-second week of pregnancy
the sound the body makes

when the child, when the knife

so do not
do not ask
me where it

is, why the
mouth stutters
when it opens

full of stale air
offers nothing
but stillborn cry.

An Open Letter to Frida Kahlo

When my legs were dumb from the D&C
when my feet were heavy, stirrupped balls of cotton
& I couldn't tell where they stopped & the blankets began,
I thought of you.
                They kept putting more blankets on me—
they were white & everyone else wore green, my doctor
in her scrubs standing between my legs. I'd been there
before, in your painting dear Frida,
& there were wires attached to my chest & there were tubes
run between my legs, & Dr. E sucked it out, him out,
my boy, I mean, & I thought if this scene were a painting
by Frida Kahlo it would be beautiful, & I laughed.
The sound filled the room like a newborn's cry.
Frida, what I wanted to say is that I understand
why you come back to this room, a hospital in Detroit,
why the paintings pin you there to the bed like a bug on a nail,
because you're still there.
                You left pieces of yourself behind—
a blot on a sheet, some tissue in a jar—& you want them back.

The Object of the Gaze

I've never seen her naked, but I know
her body like my own—
a blue ring around her drunken mouth,
the crescent of navel above the elastic of pajamas,
the shape of her legs in Downward Facing Dog.
I know we use the same brand of tampons,
that she powders her freckled chest.
In her new house, there's a box
of Depends under the sink, something
I didn't want to know about
what happened during pregnancy and birth.
This is the most intimate we've ever been,
her small son in my arms, the three of us
sticky with milk. She's bent over me
and we're both tugging wet cotton
over the baby's head, a bottleful of breastmilk
soaking his clothes, the couch cushions, me,
while her husband fastforwards
the hospital video. Her face is flushed,
and so is mine, and somehow
it wouldn't matter if there weren't a man
in the room. *I can't watch this,* she says,
the woman in the wheelchair, the newborn
in the Isolette. Her body is everywhere—
in the lens of the camera, in her son's
sucking mouth, in all of our prying eyes.

The Baby Jars, Museum of Science and Industry, 1980

This summer of roller coasters and Renaissance fairs,
my mother is pregnant
with a baby brother no bigger
than a few grains of rice, a piece of macaroni.
I'm the big girl, the big sister,
holding Daddy's hand
as we walk through the submarine
pressed against so many bodies
I can't breathe. I've never been
so afraid, lured down a coalmine
by the fuzzy chicks incubating in the foyer.
All the kids crowd around, watching them
peck through their shells, emerging
wet and matted, their eyes droopy,
uncertain. A few hours under lamplight
they start to fluff up, and I wonder
how long it took me to look normal—
a preemie in an Isolette, parents
peering at me like a science experiment
though tinted glass. Upstairs,
Daddy lifts me up so I can see
the jar babies, their pickled and waxy skin
like the skin on my dolls, with pinpricks
where I tried to pierce their ears.
The two-month embryo is hardly bigger
than my pinky finger, the five-month fetus

as long as my face. And at the end,
in the second to the last case, there's one
at thirty-four weeks, the size
I was when yellow topaz became my birthstone
instead of my mother's garnet. Its eyelids
are fused golden-gray, its mouth pursed.
And I wonder if it wants to be held
the way my mother held me,
as if I were molded of porcelain not bone,
a hand-painted miniature ready to crack.

Prayer to the New Virgin Mary

Miscarriage is nothing if not a festival of ironies.
                              —Dahlia Lithwick

Hell is AOL on a bad day, a half-finished message
on the answering machine. The word *positive*.
I stopped praying when *please let me keep her*
didn't work, when my cat shuddered and died
on the table, when the blood came, when the doctor
couldn't find the heartbeat on the sonogram.
My friend, the one with the terminal disease,
she says the Virgin Mary of the new millennium
is pregnant but she's not carrying a child, her uterus
fills with cells overgrown like bunched grapes.
She's gestating cancer instead of the Messiah.
Yes, my friend, this is the year of stumped prayers.
They shrink and sigh like pregnancy giving way.
They're left like sanitary pads in the trash, like half-filled
bottles of pills. Still, my mother goes to synagogue
each week, lights candles to honor the dead.
Prayers in a language she doesn't understand.
She tells me she likes the way the Torah looks,
the sanctuary bathed in sunlight and stained glass,
likes sharing braided loaves of bread
with old friends. What I know are these
words shuttling across cyberspace, words
like *listen*, like *I'm here*. I imagine my friend

at her big desk, sleepy dogs curled at her feet;
she sips from a mug of Lady Grey tea
and searches for answers online, her fingers
warm the words as she types.

Over the Internet

A-rated carseats and alphabet magnets;
Books on pregnancy, birth, and babycare;
Covers for shopping carts; cloth
Diapers, disinfectant, Desitin.
Email receipts and encouragement, everyone says
        you're so young, you have nothing to worry about.
Fertility guides for every blood type, a Fisher Price farm;
Grandma's Fussbuster CD for the baby who won't sleep;
Hypoallergenic formula for when the CD doesn't work;
Inflatable duckie tubs with free vinyl patches;
Jenny Lind cribs from Pottery Barn, antiqued blue.
Kindness comes on dry ice: Kosher chickens and roast beef from D.
Like you, she has lost a child. Like you, she sometimes forgets to eat.
Mother's Margarine for Passover, medical profiles of philosophers,
        chemists, twenty-one-year-old screenwriters from Napa.
Ned the Garden Gnome, a gift from Vermont for the nurse.
Ovulation test kits, with their second lines clear as an oracle;
Pink and blue pacifiers, Playtex nursing bras;
Qualitative hCG tests that never turn blue;
Roses for the hospital nightstand.
Sanitary napkins and tampons;
Thermometers and bulb syringes, tiny plastic combs.
Undergarments for new mothers, just in case.
Vial upon vial of injectable drugs, Vitex and Vitamin E.
White onesies in five different sizes;
Xytex's catalog, a xylophone;

Year's supply of Pampers from E-bay, books on
Zen and the art of infertility; plastic zoo animals
     marching two by two.

What I Never Say

The tip of my tongue is red, fiery

when I open my mouth

for the healer. Red

means anger, she says,

frustration. What I suffer

coats my tongue, slows my pulse.

Words I can't say

on the tip of the tongue

burned from Chinese tea,

words stuck in the body

when she sticks me with pins.

They spin in my palms, shiver

my abdomen with each breath.

I do not speak.

I read the map of the body

hung on her wall, red dots

for the twelve meridians,

wondering what

the needles draw out,

what she finds in me.

Dove

Her palms pray
against my spine. She lingers
at each vertebra, moving up
my ribcage with reverence
to the juncture where arm and body
kiss, the hinge of a precious door,
the Ark coveting the Torah.
She holds the solid weight
of my arm in both of hers,
I feel myself opened,
shoulder to elbow to fingertip—
warmth tingles my skin, nerves,
the whole room.

Do you feel that? she asks.
It wants to fly.

Pantoum (The Fourth April)

The tulips drooped like bruised mouths
in April rain. As I walked through them
red petals fell at my feet like blood.
Tell me it won't happen again.

In April rain, I walked through the park
holding my belly like a basket that might split.
I won't let it happen again.
That day, I sat and waited,

holding my belly like a basket
of overripe pears. I counted
days in empty vials and waited
for my body to break open—

half-gone pears on the counter,
red petals scattered in wind.
In April, my body broke open.
In April, bruised tulips and blood.

My Doctor Writes Me a Poem

I am tired
of metaphor, of translating slow ache
into grammatical sentences.

There is no syntax
for loss. There is only the word
no, dark as December sky.

There is only a diagnosis
on a medical form, a child
crossed out in my doctor's blue pen.

How do I tell her
about the blood, about the night
of shattered promises and glass?

For months I turned images
like a snowglobe in a child's hand,
waited for fat flakes to settle.

Across the table, my doctor draws
diagrams on white paper, shows me
a picture of my uterus.

See? she says
it's a poem. A poem
we have written together.

Hannah

Praise God, the midwife says,
the catheter slides like thread
through the cervix. *Praise
God*—two syllables of thanks
or a command. This morning
two blue lines on the test strip,
she raises the table
and I am carried, my
body a Torah, my feet
the handles turning, turning.
Have you prayed for a child?
No prayer in the Siddur
on my shelf, straight and blue
as a positive result.
Blessing on the Occasion
of Insemination, Blessing
for a Child Born to One.
I praise Sarah, Mother
of Infertility. I praise
Rivka and Rachel and Leah.
Yes, I have prayed. I pray
for all things new, these
million sperm swimming,
this egg an ephemeral shore.
In nine months, I will name
my daughter Hannah,
child only of prayer.

Prayer at Twenty-Three Weeks

All day she sleeps
cradled in bone
and muscle, the wings
of my pelvis around her head
like the rabbi's gentle hands

(may the lord bless you and keep you)

all day she stretches
my skin
blanketing her feet her hands
her small torso wriggling

(and grant you peace)

she goes where I go
my body
and hers, married
three vessels

connect us like woven
threads of the *tallit*.

Birth Day

Somewhere—
        a coffee shop, a bus station, a bed
in a four-room house—
            a woman is talking.

Shiver, she says. Starlight.
              There is a poem
in her, caught in her pelvis like a breech birth.

      If writers are midwives: forceps. The word
hurts—
      muscle and force, the doctor's bicep
bulging as he pulls what's been stuck in her

out. She hasn't known pain

until now. Or joy. She can't get past
this scene, the birth room, the blood.

This is the only story she will ever tell,

      how she shivered. How
      the child's wail filled the room like starlight.

My Doctor Speaks (2)

I held her skull in my hand
the fontanel like a melon
pulsing, overripe

her mother writhed
legs open as an offering
a basket of fruit about to split

again and again and again.

Still Born

The curve of my daughter's skull
is a thin purple line
under my clothes. The doctor
said before she cut me
I'd be able to wear a string bikini.
What she knew was in another place
I would have labored for days
and given birth to a girl whose head
had shrunk to fit, a small boat
swallowed in rising tide.
What she didn't say is the ache
that comes when the baby kicks.

From the Diary of a Labor and Delivery Nurse, 10 February 2004

There are days I hear nothing
but the steady gallop
of a child's heart, the lines
on the printout like footprints
at slow tide. Their mothers
resent me, my hands
inside their bodies the way
my mother scooped innards
out of Sunday chickens. But after
I cap their babies in pink and blue
the fathers take pictures and there
I am, part of the family, smiling.
I wonder when they tell the story
if they remember my name.
I wonder if they remember
anything but the shape of my hands.

Sage

The way the Rabbi hefts the Torah
on Saturday morning, she takes
the child from me, touches her
with winter-chapped hands. No
hesitation at the umbilical stump,
crusty, like a burnt offering. The baby
surrounded by soaps and potions,
I think of sacrificial altars, holy water.

When will my hands stop shaking?
Even Sarah didn't want to let go.

Maternity Ward

*The scene: a recovery room in a newly renovated American hospital. A young
mother sits, propped at a forty-five-degree angle, electrodes taped to her chest
and an oximeter on her right index finger. A nurse in blue scrubs can be seen
in the background, checking computer screens. Periodically, she palpates the
young mother's abdomen; she dozes, having spent most of the day in labor. The
baby is offstage, in a nursery the mother can't quite imagine. She is thinking
instead that it is the anniversary of the death of the poet Sylvia Plath. When
the mother falls asleep, the nurse turns her face to the audience and speaks.
Her voice is that of Plath on a 1960s radio program.*

*

You are a mother now.
In a few hours they will bring the baby
& teach you to hold her to your breast.
You tell yourself you like it
but you feel like a cow in a stall being milked:
oh yes they will milk you, the midwives
will come & they will press the tops of your breasts
& they will praise you, like a pat on a child's head.
All your life you have waited for this
for the rush of blood & water
& the pain that wrenched you in half;
you even told yourself you wanted it
this place beyond words & syntax
for hours you said no, no, no, when they offered
you potions & painkillers.

In a few days you will take the child home
& her cries will fill the apartment
& your pens will dry out
& your papers will be covered with milk
& the dishes will sit in the sink
& you will sit in blood & baby shit & vomit
& you will think of me
& you will think of the oven
& you will think of the razor blade in your jewelry box
& you will think of the children
asleep in their beds
& you will not judge.

The Cleaving

i

A cleft in my daughter's body
between milky belly and rose
of genitals, the place earth
collects when I change her diaper.
On me, it is a hairless line
that can't be wiped clean,
it is a closed mouth
that smiled at her entrance.

ii

Her birth is marked
on both our bodies
the cinnamon swirl
of her navel, cut and clamped
by the doctor's careful hand.
First, she sliced thick
layers of skin and muscle
like meat on a platter
to get her out. She leaves
an angry purple line
on my belly. Weeks
after birth, it weeps.

iii

The first time I saw
my daughter's face, slick
eyes and rosebud mouth
hours after birth, I cried.
No crowning glory burned
her entrance on my skin
just a scream that echoed
the operating room walls.
I've heard it again, at 9:32
nights when she refuses to sleep
nights my body opens
to take her back.

Maternity Leave

Body. Baby. Blood.
Words of the flesh all
I have these days. Stacks
of dirty dishes and laundry to fold,
the baby needs another diaper
and Freud sits silent
on the shelves. For six weeks
my students' teacher wears spit-stained pajamas
and I learn to let go.

Amniotic

Her belly skims the water's edge
as mine once did, pregnant
with her, a body in water
within a body in water—
now she is one, full
of formula and herself,
half her imagined adult height.
She pats her abdomen and mine
pushing my shirt up to poke
my navel. *Mama,* she says—
in an instant one becomes two
becomes one again, our bodies
severed in the birth room
as I pull her now from the bath,
head and chest and sex and legs.
I towel her off belly to belly,
and I want to hold her here forever
the solid weight of her
proof of my body's making, one
body both halved and doubled,
water and blood and air.

Emptying the Fridge, June 2005

Like sediment in years of ice
the milk in the freezer, yellows
and blues and opalescent white,
traces of the foods I ate
when I nursed her, ravenously
at first, then anorectic, meals
too meager for our doubled bodies.
The doctor said the mothers
thanked him, they'd never felt
so good as they did then, pure
on a diet of organic meats
and produce, summer ripened.
Every two hours my daughter drank
and wailed, poisoned
for months from the milk
my body leached itself to give her
and then I held her in my starved arms
and gave her a bottle and cried.

It is over now, both of us
fat and buttery,
one hundred twenty pounds
between us. I throw out eggs
and leftover Chinese, jars
of salad dressing and ketchup.

All that's left is a jug of formula,
and these useless packets of milk.
I wipe the plastic beneath them
and close the door.

On the New SIDS Prevention Guidelines

I don't know the magic
that set her heart beating
in the cave of my uterus,
that keeps it going now,
these days of fingerpaint
and stacks of blocks, books
shared in a circle of toddlers:

so I keep her with me
body and limbs blanketed
with my breath, my breasts
that once nourished her pressed
against pearls of spine:

she doesn't know the relief
I feel, lifting her
from her crib, her night-lit
room down the hall, the room
she fears monsters reside::

I fear them too, shadows
that threaten to steal her,
all the lonely breaths of her life.

First Day of Preschool

My daughter stands with her Nemo lunchbox
orange and white against the ocean of her shirt—
applesauce and algae. *No Mommy,*
she says as I come at her, preschool paparazzi,
to have something to put in her album:

in my own, I sit on the front step
blue-dressed, in thick-soled shoes,
hair tamed in pigtails.
My mother is somewhere
holding the camera, my unborn sister
kicking the curve of her uterus;
she notes how big I have gotten,
big enough for a big girl bed, big enough
for a big girl potty, big enough for school.

You till my baby? Hannah says, echoing
what I have told her for days.
She carries her lunchbox in two hands
out to the car and I strap her in,
twenty-eight pounds and forward facing
now and I wonder which one of us
is more afraid of the growing.

Cleaning

Her new school shoes
dry on paper towels
and I wipe up
yesterday's muddy footprints.

They stain the sink, the countertop,
the lap of my pants. Everything

she touches. *Dirt,*
she says, and I tell her
that she plays hard,
that's a kid's job, but

there are days
I follow her with Clorox
and a mop, erasing her
steps from the hardwood floors
fingerprints from the mirrors,
hiding toys in wicker baskets
until there is no trace.

IV

Half-Life

The maple outside my window is dying.
I tossed another negative test
into the trash this morning, one
garish pink line mocking me
with what my body has forgotten.
On my desk, an empty bowl
a dented spoon, a cracked mug.
If it is not fertilized, a human ovum
begins to decompose in 24 hours.
Does it sit in the fallopian tube
like a teenage girl waiting for her date?
Does it shimmer with anticipation?
Does it think of anything
beyond this moment of becoming?

Notes from the New
Patient Questionnaire

Begin again.

Menstrual history:
> *menarche: age 12*
> *abnormal pap smears: 1999-2001 (colposcopy; HPV-)*
> *normal ovulation; short cycles (~25 days); low progesterone/LPD*
>> *treated with prometrium (200 mg/BID)*

Begin again.

Please list all previous pregnancies and outcome:
> *D&C, 11.5 weeks, 12/02*
> *Daughter (Hannah), born 2/2004, via c/s 6 lb 12 oz*
> *~~Other experiences involving blood and tissue and questionable~~*
> *~~test results; they're real to me even if you~~*
> *~~don't want to put them in my chart; no,~~*
> *~~I don't want to see a therapist~~*

Begin again.

Past infertility treatment:
> *6/02-8/02 –3 unmedicated IUI*
> *8/02-10/02–3 Clomid (1 poss. chemical pg; 1 SAB/D&C)*
> *2/03-5/03–2 Repronex, 1 Clomid, 1 unmedicated*
>> *(daughter)*

8/08-12/08–2 unmedicated, 2 Clomid (current cycle
other clinic, 9dpo)

Begin again.

Sexual history:
Frequency of intercourse: n/a (donor)
Lubricants: n/a (donor)
Other sexual problems or concerns: n/a (donor)

Note: 36 y.o.
4 samples in lab; schedule app't with andrologist
plan: Femara 2.5 mg cd 2-6, 3 cycles; if no pg,
discuss IVF;
rec. acupuncture, reduce stress

dx: ovarian dysfunction 256.9, dysmenorrhea
625.3 (LPD); APA+
Insurance: BCBS

Begin again.

The Andrologist

She always wanted to be a boy, admired their shirtless chests in the summer when she was bound by a bra. They had swagger, bravado, their jean shorts slung low on skinny hips. The bottle of beer they held to their lips. She is one of them now, cocksure as she pulls the vial from the tank. In the waiting room, patients sit in their chairs, patiently, waiting for her. She spins the vial, lets the dead matter sink to the bottom. It's pretty in pink, like the waiting women, brushing their hair, fixing their lipstick, reading *American Baby*. She escorts them down the hall, leads them like a first date. Behind the door, they will undress. In the lab, she watches them swim.

An Open Letter to Our Sperm Donor

Our daughter looks like me
   people say, the architecture
of her eyebrows and pointed stare.
   But in the photograph of you
at thirteen months: our baby's
   toothless grin after she's grabbed
the cat by the tail. Every child
   you said needs a mother who reads
and each night I let her suck
   thick cardboard illustrations,
Big Red Barn and *Goodnight Moon*,
   while I balance her on my lap.
If you lived with us, you
   would know this. Perhaps
you would bring me a cup of tea
   while I nurse her on the couch,
a book of poems open nearby.
   Sometimes I wonder if you wonder
about us, when you're at work
   in the laboratory or when
you're feeding your new son a bottle.
   The stories of our children
are woven together. The tapestry
   couldn't be more beautiful, filled
with these widening holes.

Even her fingers feel heavy,
my sister stretched against
the walls of her womb
while my father takes pictures
because that's what fathers do
when their daughters turn three.
In the photograph, I am ponytailed
and happy, hugging a stuffed dog
bigger than my twentysome pounds,
but no one says they stopped talking
the day I died and was born.
In a year he will leave on business
and never come home. This prelude to
loss pinches my mother's face
like Passover's bitter herb.
At night she dreams of riding a motorcycle
past fields and towns until she's back home
in Jersey, eating Kosher chicken
off my grandmother's delicate plates.
She can't spend the rest of her life here
hemmed in by corn and child's toys.
Even the stripes of the wallpaper
imprison her. Even the two
daughters she loves more than choice.
When the guests arrive, she serves
cake and a crescent smile. My father puts
another roll of film in the camera.

Rock-a-bye

Like the boy in the child's rhyme
my uncle came tumbling down
two stories from his cradle
and lived to tell the tale.
It's Thanksgiving or Yom Kippur,
what's left of the family gathered
around a table cluttered with excess
and Grandma's demitasse, each
of us with a different cup and saucer,
each with a story of when and where
she picked it up, how she got that one
on clearance at Saks, that one from
her mother who brought it on the boat
from the old country. Mumbled Yiddish
words and my uncle continues
with Grandma leaving him on the balcony
because he wouldn't shut up
and she couldn't take it anymore,
Grandpa off in the Navy
and Mom kicking her belly
from the inside out. The neighbor
found him in a shrub and carried him up
to Grandma asleep on the couch.
I imagine her there with her dark curls
splayed against the pillow, mouth open
like a baby bird saying, *I'm just resting
my eyes.* We all know it's not true,

borrowed from a book and claimed
as family history, but for a moment
we're all there on a quiet street
in New Brunswick, my uncle's voice
calling all of us home.

Postcards from the Clinic (#3)

My daughter colors
during my ultrasound. *What's*
that? she wants to know

Shell

Georgia's "White Shell with Red"
      (day 3 sonogram)
on the wall behind me, on the left
      my ovaries, televised
uterus lined with swirls
      the follicles, 8 x 8, round

like O'Keeffe's shell. These days
      the world blooms red.
This painting, coil of embryo
      waiting to unfurl,
stripe of thick yellow
      a child's room bathed in light.

On the Day of IVF Retrieval,
I Walk My Daughter to the Bus

It is five years from now,
the big oak across the street
where the ash black squirrel
runs each day, leaves turning
and turned, scurrying across
my neighbor's yard; it's just past
seven in the morning when the bus
squeaks its way to a stop
the way it has every morning
for years, after the alarm, the first
cup of coffee half-drunk on the table,
years of Hannah searching the sidewalk
for dogs pulling their masters
and birds expectant at the feeder.
It is autumn in East Lansing
and the bus will drive my girl
across town to the elementary school;
she will sit three by three
on vinyl the color of fallen leaves;
she will sit, scarved and mittened
with friends, talking about Saturday
morning cartoons and video games;
and I will stay on our faded couch
waiting for the call from the clinic, thinking
how small she was once in her spring-colored shoes,
how if I listen close enough I can hear
babysteps echo the hardwood floors.

Ars Poetica

As the world awakens you sit straightbacked at your desk. Coffee
brews, and breakfast. The smell wafts up the stairs.
Coffee, the computer, maybe a pen. If you were Billy Collins
details like these would unfurl into something magical,
each blue Bic pen entering the realm of the symbolic:
French croissants and the curve of the moon. For now
greatness is as far off as the moon in the sky. The question
how to write a poem. Consult Donald Hall, Mary Oliver,
interrogate all the authorities and still, here you are,
just a young poet struggling, a handful of syllables.
K sticks in your throat. Kestrel, kingfisher.
Line by pathetic line, the poem limps along, a hard labor. This
metaphor comes from the only place that matters, the baby
nestled in its mother's pelvis, the midwife urging the body to
open. You can hear her moaning *oh-oh-oh-oooh,*
perineum stretching, the push splitting her in two. No
quest here, no *Cantos*, no *Paterson*, not even a *Prelude*, or
Richard Hugo's *Triggering Town*. Reproduction, not
sex or romance. It's embryos in petri dishes,
trigger shots of gonadotropin, test after test after test.
Ultimately maybe that's all we can ever ask for, some
vials of blood, dark tubes rolled in the nurse's hands.
When you're stuck—like now—you go back to conception
x meets x and nine months later, a girl is born.
Your hands are greedy, you want to hold her, the camera
zooms in on the young mother's face and stops

zooms out to the hospital room, the snow on the windows,
yellow balloons, vases flush with daffodils. You haven't had s-e-
x in so long you've forgotten how the body moves, the creamy
white of your skin against your lover's. Wordsworth writes of the
vale, the river, the mountain, nature as the source of the sublime—
under the poet's spell the world becomes metaphor
tenor humming against vehicle like a bird ready to take flight.
Still, you sit here, pecking out words, letting the syllables
roll in your mouth like stones. It's that flat gray of winter
quiet when nothing ever happens, when you wait
patiently, for a delivery truck, for the stick to turn blue, ping of
ovulation when anything is possible, a spark in the ovary,
nestling embryo, nights when you dream of possibility,
menses marked on the calendar in pink, your wait
longer than you ever dreamed. You fiddle, try your hand at
kyrielle, villanelle, sonnet, sestina, you'll try anything.
Just start. Jump right in. Don't think too hard.
Infertility begets infertility. Remember this in the
Harmony Room, where the doctor
guides your legs into the stirrups, says *you'll*
feel my touch, and she is so tender
every nerve in your body begins to hum and
despite everything, despite months of failure and rejection, *this*
could work. In two weeks the stick could turn
blue, in nine months, a baby, a book
a single-celled wish. Amen.

Secondary Infertility

The phone calls come
when I'm in class
when I'm in the checkout lane at the grocery
when I'm in a parent-teacher conference
when we're at a park playing with friends.
No, it is not a good time to talk.

Collage / Voice Mail

Hey, Robin, I'm sorry to call so late. I just talked to the boss lady about you. Here's the gab: come in on Thursday for repeat ultrasound; you're on the books for 8:30, call back if that's a problem. Hi, Robin, I talked to Dr. G, do your hCG shot tonight at 2:30 a.m. (yes, you heard that right, I'm sorry); call us back with any questions, otherwise we'll see you on Saturday. Hi, Robin, got your test results from the lab; progesterone was 100, that's fantastic, keep your fingers crossed, I'll put you down for a beta in a week. Let us know if you want to do it closer to home. Hi, Robin. I'm sorry but your pregnancy test came back negative, call us to schedule baseline when you get your period. Hi, Robin, I'm sorry, she needs to cancel your appointment, can you come in on Tuesday instead? Hi, Robin, we called in a prescription for Femara. We called in a prescription for Ovidrel. We called in a prescription for Follistim; take 200 units at 7:00 p.m. Call us back with any questions. Hi, Robin, I'm so sorry we forgot the Ganirelix, can you come to the clinic to pick up a sample? Call us back with any questions; we're here until 7:00 tonight. Hi, Robin, I'm sorry I don't have good news; the doctor will call you herself tonight to discuss the results. I'm sorry but your pregnancy test came back negative. Hi, Robin, I'm so sorry to have to give you this news over the phone but your pregnancy test came back negative, call us with cycle day 1. Hi, Robin, I'm sorry to call so late; we just got your results, you need to start oral contraceptives tonight; call me back immediately when you get this. Hi, Robin, I'm calling from the clinic, long game of phone tag, sorry; we're still here, call us back. Robin, I'm calling from the clinic; I have some good news, your test result was positive;

unfortunately, the number is low, we'd like you to retest beta hCG on Saturday. Be sure that you're still taking Prometrium. Hi, Robin, I'm sorry but the news isn't good, your beta is going down; we'd like to retest. Hey, Robin . . . it's Doctor G; I've been thinking a lot about you. I really want to talk to you. I'll try you on your other number.

My Daughter Asks for a Baby Sister from the Tooth Fairy

In the photograph, she wears a yellow dress with a bow
to her preschool graduation; she stands
with her classmates and teacher, smiling wide.
She lost her first tooth last week. I put it
in an envelope in my nightstand, where I keep
test results and baby socks, good-luck charms.
I slipped a gold coin under her pillow while she slept.
Today I stand with the other mothers
with their babies in strollers, in slings, my uterus
a clenched fist. I will not be having a child
in January. I will not be having a child
before my daughter turns six. Yesterday
my doctor scrawled *recurrent pregnancy loss,*
sent me for a blood draw. This
is what I carry with me. What I want
is to smash glass. What I want is to drink myself
into oblivion. But I take her out for ice cream,
go to the bathroom, change my pad.

I Am Sorry for Your Loss

Listen to my words: when I say "anonymous"
I mean I do not know him
literally

not that I do not want to say his name but that
he is unnamable, so it says "none"
on the birth certificate in the state of Texas

as the woman from the hospital called to double check
while I was sitting in the rocker with my two-week old and weeping
incision.

No, that wasn't a mistake.
When I say "single mother by choice," I do not mean
"by default" or "by chance"—I was not fucked

after getting drunk in a bar, I did not get knocked up
by a boyfriend who wasn't ready to father. No,
I sat in a room with a glass of merlot and thumbed

pages of essays. My number is 6666. My number is 0371.
Reproduction is not romance when it is done in a lab.

This does not make me "emotional"::

If you want to see me cry, can we talk instead
about what it was like to drive 70 miles roundtrip
2, 3, 8, 10 days a month to have my ovaries
examined, to be pricked and prodded, to bleed, to lose
a child. My chart says "dilation and curettage."
My chart says "missed abortion." Go ahead: ask
my doctor what it was like to operate while I sobbed.

:: and, if you ask my daughter if she is sad

because she has a "donor" not a "father,"
she would tell you she was made by "Irish seeds"
and that makes her happy on Saint Patrick's Day.

This is my lexicon: antiphospholipid syndrome, anti-
coagulation therapy, MTHFR mutation, recurrent miscarriage,
high-risk. Happy Pregnancy and Infant Loss Remembrance Day.

In Lieu of a Baby Book

First trip to the fertility clinic
First insemination
First injection
First IVF
First ultrasound
First trip to the hospital
First child
First loss

V-Day 2011

There is a poem in this girl
walking into class, a red bow
in her hair, her v-neck blouse and
flouncy skirt. She is beautiful, festive,
and I want to capture all that she is
and package it and savor it like bonbons.
It is Valentine's Day and tomorrow
will be cycle day 1 and it will all start
then, this exchanging of DNA, some
lovely twenty-something's eggs
retrieved from her ovaries and glinting
in a petri dish, embryonic corona
my child. It matters that she could be
my student who writes poems,
who tells me something I didn't know
about love and generosity, and I feel it
pulsing in my uterus, in this space
flush with possibility, as I sip my tea
feeling the weight of my age. And how
innocent she is of her body's loveliness,
its pink sex, all that it can do.

Pregnancy after Loss

i

A boy empties a white pail
into flames on my television
and my hand holds that place
it never left. I watch and wonder
what happened to my son
when the doctor wrenched him
from my body too small
to be seen on the sonogram
but big enough to swell
my whole world. My breasts
my belly even my heart
sore from pumping blood
to his stumped cells. After
when I was back in the bed
with Raggedy Ann legs
she asked if I was stubborn
the way a mother might ask
another woman's child. My uterus
clenched around what wasn't there
and wouldn't let go. Then
she put her hand on my forehead
and we were two women
who had created a child together
and there are no words to say
what passed between us.

ii

Those snow-covered weeks
before surgery, I saw
my son in the backseat of the car
looking out an airplane window
asking for French toast in the morning.
I am not a person who has visions
I am not a person who believes in ghosts
or even God. But this dark-haired boy
who held my hand when we crossed the street
only he could have been my son. *Benjamin*.

iii

I refuse to pretend
my son is an angel
on a fat cloud watching over me.

iv

Once I imagined dressing him
in tiny t-shirts swimming in ducks,
floppy hats that tie under the chin.
I would have taken him to the park
I would have spent the summer
I would have
I

V

*Women talk about their pregnancies
not their miscarriages.* Words whispered
under the hum of fluorescent bulbs
while what was left poured out of me
onto white sheets. It is nine years later
and my body opens like a sieve:
a jumble of bloody syllables.

The Childless Woman Has a Baby

Yes, it's true. 3:00 a.m. in the rocking chair, his tiny fist pulsing your breast like a mama cat, suck-suck-swallow. The purple gash of the bikini line. And yet. Your ovaries knotted to that old self with a pomegranate thread, the bracelet that says *I survived*. When you take him to Baby Time at the library, when you sit in the pediatrician's waiting room, when you wheel his stroller through the shopping mall, you are unremarkable. The sleepy corners of your eyes, the messy ponytail, milky spit-up on the shirt. But you carry that old self with you, heavier than anything in the diaper bag. In those dark hours you rock back and forth, the lullabies heave in your chest.

Postcards from the Clinic (#4)

I hold the baby
in the waiting room, tell him
we're going to see god.

Lexicon

Yes, it is possible to be a little bit pregnant

two lines don't add up
to a baby where I live

sometimes a line isn't really—
infertility like special 3D glasses in movie theaters
you need to be a long term patient
to see some things, pink shadows
on day 9 First Response—

but all those waiting room hours
work well at night in the rocking chair
when I recount every blasted
conversation in your office

      FSH, AMH, E2, P4, beta HCG
      Lovenox, Folgard, Medrol,
      diminished ovarian reserve, recurrent
      pregnancy loss, vanishing twin,
      clotting disorder, two
      day 5 blastocysts on ice

All I got for 60K worth of treatment
was a baby
to put in this stupid onesie.

Oh, the joys of the petri dish. Black
black humor. What can I say?

27 inches and 15 lbs later
I'm still talking about it—
blood on the floor, dead babies, the whole
shebang.

Yes, I said it. Sometimes babies
—embryos fetuses babies—
die. In fallopian tubes, in utero, in
their Pottery Barn decorated cribs.

The universe owes us nothing.

I know, I know—none of this is pretty.

But when I look at that beautiful sleeping boy
with another woman's nose, his hand pulsing
my breast, I also know that infertility

taught me love
of the most pure and complicated sort. Still

I am there, with you, in the Harmony Room
my legs high in stirrups, a catheter in your hand,

and all I can give you in return
is a photograph on his birthday, this poem,
these whispered words in the dark.

Coda: Dear Doctor

It is February 2014, and I am no longer a patient. I get on the small plane and there's a woman I recognize—50ish, university sweatshirt— but can't place her. She spins in my mind, blood in a centrifuge, and there. Exam room: she's reading my file, *oh yes here*, test results from 2003, from 2009, from 2011. The old acronyms swirl up, settle like debris at the bottom of the vial. Another bandage on my left arm.

Oh yes—

My son, three weeks, sleeps in his car seat, propped up by rolled towels, a trick I learned from a friend—he is so small, barely five pounds, intrauterine growth restriction. He's beautiful, she says, he'll be fine. Just needed out of that uterus (*hostile environment* the doctor said; *why are you on heparin?* they said as I lay on the operating table, arms pinned to my sides like Jesus. Again: *How many miscarriages? No, that's not clinically significant*). Congratulations, she says, go home, enjoy the baby; you probably don't need it, but keep the Lovenox, you never know.

It is February 2014, and I am no longer a patient. I no longer clock my days by injections and pills. But it returns. In a face on a plane. In a phone call from the clinic about those leftover embryos—use, donate, destroy. Please sign the forms. It's time.

Notes

In these poems I have deliberately left "untranslated" many of the acronyms and insurance diagnostic codes that patients encounter—a way of performing the often alienating effects of routine life at the fertility clinic. Should you care to do further research, the website run by RESOLVE: The National Infertility Association is a useful resource, as is the blog Stirrup Queens, a clearinghouse of adoption, loss, and infertility blogs run by Melissa Ford, author of *Navigating the Land of If: Understanding Infertility and Exploring Your Options*.

"The Childless Women Talk about Frida Kahlo": Although the account is fictionalized, details of Frida Kahlo's life are drawn from *Frida: A Biography of Frida Kahlo*, by Hayden Herrera, as well as the film *Frida* (2002); images are borrowed from her self-portraits, including "Frida and the Abortion," "The Henry Ford Hospital," "My Birth," "Self-Portrait As a Tehuana," and "My Nurse and I."

"Prayer to the New Virgin Mary": The idea of the New Virgin Mary comes from Amy Tudor. This poem is dedicated to her.

"Pregnancy after Loss": The opening image comes from the film *The Cider House Rules* (1999).

Acknowledgments

Like most good things in my life, this book was a long time in the making and inseparable from the events that inspired it. I am deeply grateful to the poet friends and teachers who encouraged this work in various incarnations: Janine Certo, Mark Doty, Telaina Eriksen, Stephanie Glazier, Erin Radcliffe, Kristen Renzi, Maura Stanton, and Amy Tudor. And to those who accompanied me on this long journey: Jennifer Allswede, Zarena Aslami, Jesse and Eden Bendorf, Alissa Cohen, Lynn Chindlund, Melissa Fore, Melissa Hidalgo, Walton Muyumba, Elena Olivé, Kristina Quynn, Bonnie Roos, Mindy Silbergleid, Terrie Stainman, and the many pseudonymous members of the ALI blogosphere. Thanks to publisher Joan Cusack Handler for her support. To Ellen Wilson and L. April Gago, there are no words. This book is for them, and for Hannah and Hayden.

I am also grateful to the following journals and anthologies in which these poems first appeared, sometimes in different forms or with different titles:

> *Crab Orchard Review:* "Over the Internet"
> *Fertile Source:* "Miscarriage (3)," "Pregnancy after Loss"
> *Fifth Wednesday Journal:* "The Baby Jars, Museum of Science and Industry, 1980"
> *Folio:* "The Childless Women Talk about Frida Kahlo"
> *Hospital Drive:* "From the Diary of a Labor and Delivery Nurse," "Three Aprils"
> *Mom Egg Review:* "Sage"
> *Prose-Poem Project:* "After the Miscarriage, My Doctor Speaks"

Rattle: "An Open Letter to Our Sperm Donor"

River Oak Review: "Prayer at Twenty-Three Weeks," "The Object of the Gaze"

Women.Period: "I Draw My Doctor a Picture"

Versions of "The Childless Women Talk about Frida Kahlo," "Miscarriage (3)," and "An Open Letter to Frida Kahlo" also appear in the chapbook *Frida Kahlo, My Sister* (Finishing Line Press, 2014).

CavanKerry's Mission

CavanKerry Press is committed to expanding the reach of poetry to a general readership by publishing poets whose works explore the emotional and psychological landscapes of everyday life.

Other Books in the LaurelBooks Series